Families Navigating Global Transitions

TEENS COMPANION

JENI WARD & KATH WILLIAMS

First Edition 2025

© COPYRIGHT INTERWOVEN 2025

All rights reserved. No part of this publication may be reproduced, stored in or introduced into a Retrieval system; or be transmitted, in any form, or by any means (electronic, mechanical, photocopying, recording or otherwise) without the prior written permission of the publisher. This book is sold, subject to the condition that is shall not by way or trade or otherwise, be lent, resold hired out, or otherwise circulate without the publisher's prior consent, in any form of binding or cover other than that in which it is published and without a similar condition, including this condition, being imposed on the subsequent purchaser.

ISBN paperback: 978-0-6457886-0-0

This edition was published in Aberfoyle Park by Mission Interlink in April 2025

Illustrations by:
River by Emma Elliot page 10

Typesetting by: Kath Williams
Cover layout by: Jeni Ward & Kath Williams

✈ Contents

🌟 Getting Started
About Us 5
Introduction 6
Mood Tracker 7
The River 8
Important Dates & Birthdays 9
Contacts 10

📅 Preparing for the Move
12 Months Ahead 12
9 Months Ahead 18
6 Months Ahead 24
3 Months Ahead 30
1 Month Ahead 36
1 Week Ahead 42
Travel Day 48

🏠 Settling In
1 Week After 54
1 Month After 60
3 Months After 66
6 Months After 72
9 Months After 78
12 Months After 84

👍 Tip Sheet : Preparing for a New Country...... 90

INTERWOVEN

Interwoven is a Missions Interlink Ministry, created through a partnership of dedicated workers with a passion for nurturing Third Culture Kids, ensuring their physical, spiritual, and mental well-being on the field. Our primary mission is to develop resources that directly engage Third Culture Kids. Additionally, we aim to support and provide valuable resources to those who work with and care for them.

KATH WILLIAMS (ISV AUSTRALIA)

Kath is a dedicated and professional social worker with a profound passion for supporting Third Culture Kids (TCKs) in their growth and development. Currently, she works with TCKs through two mission organizations in Australia. Kath is the co-author of "Navigating a Global Transition Again: A Journey of Faith" and "Thongs or Flip Flops: A Book for Aussie TCKs."

With 20 years of experience working with children and teens, Kath's diverse background includes work with Indigenous communities, foster children, and community camp-sites. She spent two years in Cambodia, where she contributed to the student support team at Hope International School and volunteered with middle and high school students at a local international church youth group.

Outside of her professional life, Kath enjoys going out for coffee and food with friends, exploring with her camera, visiting zoos, reading, listening to music, and traveling as much as she can.

JENI WARD

Jeni Ward is a Third Culture Kid (TCK) whose journey has taken her across diverse landscapes including Ethiopia, South Sudan, Canada, and Australia. With over 13 years of experience in cross-cultural ministry, Jeni has dedicated her life to understanding and bridging the gaps between different cultures. As a lifelong learner, she is passionate about walking alongside other TCKs, offering guidance, support, and a deep sense of community.

As a founding member of Interwoven, an organization dedicated to developing materials and resources for TCKs (and the producer of this book). Through her work with Interwoven, she has been instrumental in creating resources that address the unique challenges and opportunities that come with a multicultural upbringing. These include God in the Mess and God in the Cracks. As well as co-authoring "Navigating a Global Transition Again: A Journey of Faith" All this together with Kath Williams. Check these great resources out at https://www.interwovenglobal.com .

Her commitment to this cause reflects not just in her professional life, but also in her everyday interactions, where she continuously seeks to connect, inspire, and empower those around her through coaching and debriefing.

🌟 Welcome to Your Companion Journal

Hey,
This journal is just for you.
While your family might be using a big planner to get ready for your move, this book is your personal space to process everything you're thinking and feeling along the way.

Moving to a new country can be exciting, but it can also feel overwhelming, confusing, or even a bit lonely at times. This journal is here to help you make sense of it all—whether you're looking forward to the change or feeling unsure about what's ahead.

💡 How to Use This Journal

You can work through this journal at your own pace. Each section matches part of your journey—before the move, during travel, and after you've arrived. You'll find:

- Practical pages – to help you think through what's changing and what matters most to you
- Heart pages – space to reflect on your emotions, relationships, and identity
- Creative prompts – to write, doodle, or get your thoughts out visually
- "Tell a friend" or "Share with someone" sections – to help you connect, if you want to
- Fun activities – from memory pages and reflection games to creativity boosters
- "Wreck This Page" – a space for you to let loose and be real—rip, draw, splash, or journal whatever's on your mind
- Mood tracker – to check in with how you're feeling across the weeks or months

  There's no pressure to complete every page, and no one way to use it:
  ✔ Use it regularly—or just when you feel like it
  ✔ Keep it private—or share parts with someone you trust
  ✔ Add your own pages, journal entries, or artwork

Mood Tracker

A mood tracker allows each member a chance to track whether they are feeling happy, sad, tired, angry, bored, etc.

- Blue- Sad
- Red- Angry
- Yellow – Happy
- Green- Anxious
- Orange- Worried
- Purple- Scared

Make your code here then contribute to your families planner

🌀 The River: A Way to Check In

Picture your move like a river.

One side is where you've come from—everything familiar.
The other side is where you're heading—a new environment, new routines, maybe even a new version of yourself.
The river in between is transition: that space where change happens.

Some days the water feels calm, steady, maybe even exciting.
Other days it's more like rough currents, unexpected turns, or feeling stuck in the middle with no clear way forward.

That's normal.

Everyone in your family is somewhere on that river.
Some might feel like they're already settling in.
Others might still be figuring it out.
You don't all have to be in the same place.

The river can be a helpful way to check in—with yourself and with others.

🗣️ You can ask:
- What's helping me stay afloat right now?
- Do I feel like I'm drifting, paddling hard, or coasting?
- Am I still in the middle—or starting to see the other side?

🎨 Activity: Draw your own version of the river. Where are you in it today? Are there rocks, whirlpools, still water, or sunshine? Is anyone else in your boat?

You don't have to know all the answers.

This picture can help you talk to your family about what's really going on inside. You don't have to figure it out all at once—but the river can help you notice where you are.

You Can Draw Your River here

Important dates & Birthdays

Contacts

Name	Socials	Phone

12 Months Ahead : Meet Me

Before anything starts changing, this is your chance to check in with who you are right now—where you live, what you care about, and what's on your mind as you look ahead.

This is your starting point.

My name:

My age right now:

Countries I've lived in:

Where I live now feels like

What I'll miss most when I leave:

What I won't miss:

A place, person, or routine that's part of my everyday life:

Something I hope people here will remember about me:

One thing I'm curious (or unsure) about when I think of what's next:

Something I'm looking forward to:

Practical

I WISH
☐ I wish I could pause time for a bit—just to take it all in.

I THINK
☐ I think I need to start preparing for change—even if it's just little steps.

Heart

TELL A FRIEND
☐ Tell a friend one thing you're excited or nervous about.

SHARE WITH SOMEONE
☐ Share with someone a memory or place that feels important to you right now.

MOOD TRACKER

☐	☐	☐	☐	☐	Week 1
☐	☐	☐	☐	☐	Week 2
☐	☐	☐	☐	☐	Week 3
☐	☐	☐	☐	☐	Week 4
☐	☐	☐	☐	☐	Week 5
☐	☐	☐	☐	☐	Week 6
☐	☐	☐	☐	☐	Week 7
☐	☐	☐	☐	☐	Week 8
☐	☐	☐	☐	☐	Week 9
☐	☐	☐	☐	☐	Week 10
☐	☐	☐	☐	☐	Week 11
☐	☐	☐	☐	☐	Week 12

NOTES:

NOTES:

Pictures of where you live

Create a symbol, logo, or collage that represents who you are right now. It could include places, values, music, hobbies, or anything else that helps express your identity before the move.

9 Months Ahead : Looking Around

You're still where you've been living, but maybe the move is starting to feel more real. You might be making memories, trying to enjoy what's left, or feeling like you're living in two places at once—mentally already thinking about what's ahead.

This is a time to notice, appreciate, and reflect on the life you're still in.

What are some things I don't want to forget about this place?

Who do I want to spend more time with before I go?

What feels like "everyday life" here—but might be totally different later?

A routine or small moment that's meaningful to me:

Something I've learned or grown in over the last year:

What's something that still feels unfinished or unresolved?

Practical

I WISH

☐ I wish I could freeze this one part of my life for just a little longer.

I THINK

☐ I think I should start making a list of people and places I want to say good-bye to well.

Heart

TELL A FRIEND

☐ something you'll miss that they might not know about.

SHARE WITH SOMEONE

☐ a memory you want to hold onto.

MOOD TRACKER

☐	☐	☐	☐	☐	Week 1
☐	☐	☐	☐	☐	Week 2
☐	☐	☐	☐	☐	Week 3
☐	☐	☐	☐	☐	Week 4
☐	☐	☐	☐	☐	Week 5
☐	☐	☐	☐	☐	Week 6
☐	☐	☐	☐	☐	Week 7
☐	☐	☐	☐	☐	Week 8
☐	☐	☐	☐	☐	Week 9
☐	☐	☐	☐	☐	Week 10
☐	☐	☐	☐	☐	Week 11
☐	☐	☐	☐	☐	Week 12

NOTES:

NOTES:

Create a "snapshot" page—draw or write about a moment from this week that you'd want to keep in your memory. It doesn't have to be big or exciting—just something real.

Photos of the Places you will miss ?

6 Months Ahead : Getting Real

Six months might still sound like a while, but things may be starting to shift—your thoughts, friendships, or how you feel about the move. It's a mix of holding on and getting ready.

Let's pause and think about where you're at right now.

What has started to feel different recently?

Something I'm glad I still get to enjoy for a bit longer:

A relationship I'm not sure how to say goodbye to:

Something I want to do before I leave:

What helps me feel grounded when things feel uncertain:

Practical

I WISH

☐ I wish I could slow down time just a little

I THINK

☐ I think I need to start planning how I want to say goodbye to people and places.

Heart

TELL A FRIEND

☐ what you're starting to feel as the move gets closer.

SHARE WITH SOMEONE

☐ what you're worried about losing—or what you're holding on to.

MOOD TRACKER

☐	☐	☐	☐	☐	Week 1
☐	☐	☐	☐	☐	Week 2
☐	☐	☐	☐	☐	Week 3
☐	☐	☐	☐	☐	Week 4
☐	☐	☐	☐	☐	Week 5
☐	☐	☐	☐	☐	Week 6
☐	☐	☐	☐	☐	Week 7
☐	☐	☐	☐	☐	Week 8
☐	☐	☐	☐	☐	Week 9
☐	☐	☐	☐	☐	Week 10
☐	☐	☐	☐	☐	Week 11
☐	☐	☐	☐	☐	Week 12

NOTES:

NOTES:

BUCKET LIST

Make a "bucket list" for this place—realistic or creative. Include places to go, people to hang out with, or even small things like a favourite food you want to eat again.

Make a packaging collage of your favourite labels

3 Months Ahead : It's Getting Close

Now the move is starting to feel real. Maybe boxes are showing up. Goodbyes are being planned. You might feel excited, overwhelmed, numb, or all of that at once.

Let's check in before things get too busy.

What parts of the move are starting to happen around me?

What's been said or done recently that made it feel more "real"?

One thing I've already started to let go of:

One thing I haven't figured out how to say goodbye to yet:

How is my body reacting lately—am I tired, tense, wired, or calm?

What's something that's giving me energy or joy right now?

Practical

I WISH

☐ I wish I had more time with _____.

I THINK

☐ I think I need to start being intentional about how I spend the next few weeks.

Heart

TELL A FRIEND

☐ something you're already missing, even before you've left.

SHARE WITH SOMEONE

☐ one thing you hope they'll remember about you.

MOOD TRACKER

☐	☐	☐	☐	☐	Week 1
☐	☐	☐	☐	☐	Week 2
☐	☐	☐	☐	☐	Week 3
☐	☐	☐	☐	☐	Week 4
☐	☐	☐	☐	☐	Week 5
☐	☐	☐	☐	☐	Week 6
☐	☐	☐	☐	☐	Week 7
☐	☐	☐	☐	☐	Week 8
☐	☐	☐	☐	☐	Week 9
☐	☐	☐	☐	☐	Week 10
☐	☐	☐	☐	☐	Week 11
☐	☐	☐	☐	☐	Week 12

NOTES:

NOTES:

Wreck the page

There are no rules here—just fun! This is YOUR page to do something wild, silly, or messy. Ready? Pick one or more of these challenges and go for it!

🖍️ Draw with your eyes closed!
Can you guess what you made?

✂️ Tear off a corner of the page.
Then tape it back on in a weird place!

👟 Step on this page with your sock.
Leave a footprint! (Don't worry, you can wash your socks.)

🎨 Scribble in ALL your favorite colors.
No lines—just wild color!

🍕 Pretend this page is your favorite food.
Draw it, decorate it, or fold it like a sandwich!

📦 Crumple the page up into a ball.
Then flatten it back out. Now what does it look like?

⭐ Make a mini collage.
Glue on pieces of wrapping paper, stickers, magazine scraps, or leaves you find outside.

✋ Trace your hand
...then turn it into an animal, monster, or superhero!

🌀 Spin in a circle, then draw something while you're dizzy!
(Only if it's safe and you're not near anything breakable!)

Wreck the page

1 Months Ahead : The Final Countdown

It's really happening.

One month might feel like no time at all—or way too long. You're probably juggling final plans, last hangouts, packing, and a lot of mixed emotions. This is a time to slow down, notice what you need, and prepare your heart as much as your suitcase.

What still feels unfinished or unsaid?

A place I want to visit one more time:

Someone I still want to spend time with:

One thing I want to leave behind well:

Something I want to bring with me (physically or emotionally):

If I could freeze a moment from this place, it would be:

Something that's helping me feel grounded this week:

Practical

I WISH
☐ I wish I had more time to say goodbye the way I want to.

I THINK
☐ I think I need to start giving myself permission to let go.

Heart

TELL A FRIEND
☐ Tell a friend one thing you've loved about your time here.

SHARE WITH SOMEONE
☐ Share with someone a fear or hope you haven't talked about yet.

MOOD TRACKER
☐ ☐ ☐ ☐ ☐ Week 1
☐ ☐ ☐ ☐ ☐ Week 2
☐ ☐ ☐ ☐ ☐ Week 3
☐ ☐ ☐ ☐ ☐ Week 4

NOTES:

NOTES:

Plan your Goodbye Party
Who do you want there ? What do you want to do ?

Create a visual "memory board" — draw, collage, or list things you want to take with you in your heart: smells, sounds, people, feelings, moments.

1 Week Ahead : Almost there

You're in the final week.

It's probably busy. There might be goodbye events, last-minute packing, or random waves of emotion. It's okay if you're not sure how to feel—or if you feel everything at once.

Let this page be a place to pause, even just for a moment.

Something I still need to do (logistically):

Something I still need to do (emotionally):

A moment from this week I want to hold on to:

Someone I said goodbye to—what was that like?

Something I'm nervous about as the move gets closer:

Something I'm holding onto that gives me strength:

Practical

I WISH
☐ I wish I had a little more time to soak this all in.

I THINK
☐ I think I need to focus on what matters most this week.

Heart

TELL A FRIEND
☐ Tell a friend something that helped you during this past season.

SHARE WITH SOMEONE
☐ Share with someone what you're going to miss the most.

MOOD TRACKER

☐ ☐ ☐ ☐ ☐ Day 1
☐ ☐ ☐ ☐ ☐ Day 2
☐ ☐ ☐ ☐ ☐ Day 3
☐ ☐ ☐ ☐ ☐ Day 4
☐ ☐ ☐ ☐ ☐ Day 5
☐ ☐ ☐ ☐ ☐ Day 6
☐ ☐ ☐ ☐ ☐ Day 7

NOTES:

NOTES:

PLAY LIST

**Create a play-list or song list for this week.
What songs match your mood, your memories, or what you want to remember from this season?**

Create a map of where you currently live ?

Travel Day : In Between Everything

This is the in-between.

You've said your goodbyes. You've packed the bags. Now you're on the way—airports, car rides, long flights, maybe a layover, maybe some tears. It's a strange mix of motion and waiting, holding on and letting go.

You might feel excited, exhausted, sad, numb—or all of those at once.

Take a moment to notice where you are inside, not just where you're going on the outside.

How did saying goodbye feel today?

Something that surprised me:

A moment I want to remember from this day:

A moment I want to forget:

A small thing that helped me feel calm:

What I saw or heard that felt meaningful (song, photo, message, prayer):

Practical

I WISH
☐ I wish I could keep part of today with me.

I THINK
☐ I think I need rest before I can figure out what I feel.

Heart

TELL A FRIEND
☐ Tell a friend what felt hardest about today.

SHARE WITH SOMEONE
☐ Share with someone one thing you're carrying forward in your heart.

MOOD TRACKER

☐	☐	☐	☐	☐	Day 1
☐	☐	☐	☐	☐	Day 2
☐	☐	☐	☐	☐	Day 3
☐	☐	☐	☐	☐	Day 4
☐	☐	☐	☐	☐	Day 5
☐	☐	☐	☐	☐	Day 6
☐	☐	☐	☐	☐	Day 7

NOTES:

NOTES:

Travel Snapshot

Write or sketch a "travel snapshot"—one moment from today that felt important, weird, beautiful, or hard. It could be a photo in your mind, a sentence you heard, or something you noticed through the window.

Airport Bingo

Someone Sleeping	Wearing a backpack	Wearing a bright shirt
Airplane taking off	A flight attendant	Duty Free counter
Has a neck pillow	Suitcase with stickers	Can see our flight status on the board
Someone face-timing	Sign in Another language	Child wearing headphones

1 week After: First Impressions

You've arrived.

The place might still feel unfamiliar. Or maybe you've already found a few things that feel okay—or even kind of exciting. You might be tired, curious, overwhelmed, or just trying to make it through each day. All of that is normal.

Take a few moments to reflect on what this first week has been like.

What was your first impression of this place?

One thing that felt completely new:

One thing that felt familiar:

A moment that felt really strange or unexpected:

Someone who has been kind to you so far:

A part of the day that's been easiest... and one that's been hardest:

Practical 🔧

I WISH

☐ I wish I knew how to do _____ already.

I THINK

☐ I think I need more time to settle before I figure everything out.

Heart 💛

TELL A FRIEND

☐ Tell a friend one thing that surprised you about this place.

SHARE WITH SOMEONE

☐ Share with someone what you're missing the most right now.

MOOD TRACKER

☐	☐	☐	☐	Day 1
☐	☐	☐	☐	Day 2
☐	☐	☐	☐	Day 3
☐	☐	☐	☐	Day 4
☐	☐	☐	☐	Day 5
☐	☐	☐	☐	Day 6
☐	☐	☐	☐	Day 7

NOTES:

NOTES:

Draw or describe your "first week photo album." Pick three moments—funny, awkward, memorable, or emotional—and write a caption for each.

Wreck It Page

1 Month After: Finding Your Rhythm

You've been here a month now.

Some things might still feel unfamiliar—but maybe others are starting to make more sense. This stage is often when the adrenaline fades and the real adjustment begins. You might feel a little more steady... or a little more tired. Or both.

Let's check in on what life is like one month in:

One small win from this month:

A habit or routine I'm starting to get used to:

Something I didn't expect to miss—but I do:

Something I've started to enjoy here:

A challenge I'm still figuring out:

One thing I'm proud of myself for:

Practical 🔧

I WISH

☐ I wish I could skip ahead and know how this is all going to turn out.

I THINK

☐ I think I'm slowly starting to find my way—even if it's not easy.

Heart

TELL A FRIEND

☐ Tell a friend something you've discovered about yourself this month.

SHARE WITH SOMEONE

☐ Share with someone what's helped you get through the harder days.

MOOD TRACKER

☐ ☐ ☐ ☐ ☐ Week 1
☐ ☐ ☐ ☐ ☐ Week 2
☐ ☐ ☐ ☐ ☐ Week 3
☐ ☐ ☐ ☐ ☐ Week 4
☐ ☐ ☐ ☐ ☐ Week 5
☐ ☐ ☐ ☐ ☐ Week 6
☐ ☐ ☐ ☐ ☐ Week 7
☐ ☐ ☐ ☐ ☐ Week 8

NOTES:

NOTES:

Create a map of where you currently live ?

Photos of your new school, home, neighbourhood

3 Month After: In the Middle of it

You're not brand new here anymore—but it might not feel familiar yet either. This is the middle zone, where things are starting to settle, but you're still figuring out where you fit and how to feel about it all.

That's okay. This part of the journey takes time.

Let's take a moment to reflect:

What's been the hardest part of adjusting lately?

What's been unexpectedly good?

How do I feel about my friendships or social life right now?

What's something I miss that still catches me off guard?

Something I've learned about the culture, people, or way of life here:

A routine that's finally feeling "normal":

Practical

I WISH
☐ I wish I could find more consistency in _____.

I THINK
☐ I think I've made more progress than I usually give myself credit for.

Heart

TELL A FRIEND
☐ Something that's changed in you over the past few months.

SHARE WITH SOMEONE
☐ Something you're still hoping for in this place.

MOOD TRACKER

☐	☐	☐	☐	☐	Week 1
☐	☐	☐	☐	☐	Week 2
☐	☐	☐	☐	☐	Week 3
☐	☐	☐	☐	☐	Week 4
☐	☐	☐	☐	☐	Week 5
☐	☐	☐	☐	☐	Week 6
☐	☐	☐	☐	☐	Week 7
☐	☐	☐	☐	☐	Week 8

NOTES:

NOTES:

3 month Snapshot

Create a "3-Month Snapshot" collage or journal entry. Include the things that feel meaningful—foods, songs, habits, challenges, places, people. Think of it like a memory board of what this season is really like.

3 Month Snapshot

6 Month After: Looking Back, Looking in

You've been here for half a year. That's a big deal.

By now, some things probably feel more settled. You've built some rhythms, maybe some friendships, and you've probably hit some walls too. It's okay to feel stretched. It's okay to feel stronger. Both can be true.

Let's take a look at where you are now:

Something that used to feel hard but is now easier:

A moment I felt proud recently:

Something I still feel unsure or disconnected about:

How have I changed since arriving here?

What part of me still feels the same?

A small win I want to acknowledge:

Practical 🔧

I WISH

☐ I wish I could explain this transition to someone who's never moved.

I THINK

☐ I think I'm learning more about myself than I expected.

Heart 💛

TELL A FRIEND

☐ Tell a friend something you've overcome in the last six months.

SHARE WITH SOMEONE

☐ Share with someone a question you're still carrying.

MOOD TRACKER

☐	☐	☐	☐	☐	Week 1
☐	☐	☐	☐	☐	Week 2
☐	☐	☐	☐	☐	Week 3
☐	☐	☐	☐	☐	Week 4
☐	☐	☐	☐	☐	Week 5
☐	☐	☐	☐	☐	Week 6
☐	☐	☐	☐	☐	Week 7
☐	☐	☐	☐	☐	Week 8

NOTES:

NOTES:

Then and Now" Picture Frames
Draw two side-by-side boxes:

In the first one, draw a memory from your first week here

In the second one, draw something that happened this week

My "Noticing" Photo Challenge
Take pictures of 3 things that feel interesting or beautiful

1 thing that felt hard today

1 thing that made you smile

9 Month After: Not New Anymore

You're no longer the "new person," but that doesn't mean everything's easy now. At this point, you might be settling into a rhythm—or still adjusting in unexpected ways. Some days might feel hopeful. Others might feel heavy.

Nine months in is a good time to pause and notice how far you've come... and where you're still growing.

What's something I understand now that I didn't at the beginning?

What's been the most meaningful moment from the last few months?

What's one thing I've accepted that I was fighting before?

What still doesn't feel right or easy—and why?

How am I treating myself these days—am I being kind or critical?

What's one way I've changed for the better?

Practical

I WISH

☐ I wish I could go back and give myself permission to feel everything.

I THINK

☐ I think I'm stronger than I realized—even when it doesn't feel that way

Heart

TELL A FRIEND

☐ Something real about this season that you haven't said out loud.

SHARE WITH SOMEONE

☐ what you've been proud of—quietly or loudly.

MOOD TRACKER

☐	☐	☐	☐	☐	Week 1
☐	☐	☐	☐	☐	Week 2
☐	☐	☐	☐	☐	Week 3
☐	☐	☐	☐	☐	Week 4
☐	☐	☐	☐	☐	Week 5
☐	☐	☐	☐	☐	Week 6
☐	☐	☐	☐	☐	Week 7
☐	☐	☐	☐	☐	Week 8

NOTES:

NOTES:

Wreck the page

Wreck the page

12 Month After: One Year Later

You've made it through a full year in this new place.

That doesn't mean everything is perfect now—or that you've figured everything out. But it does mean you've faced big change, kept going, and grown through it. You've built a new rhythm, told your story in new ways, and kept showing up. That's something to be proud of.

Let's reflect on the journey so far:

What's one thing I never thought I'd adjust to—but I did?

What has changed the most about me over the past year?

What do I want to remember about this transition?

What do I wish I could forget—or let go of?

What still feels unresolved or in progress?

What's one hope or goal I have for the next season of life?

Practical

I WISH
☐ I wish more people understood what this year has been like for me.

I THINK
☐ I think this transition has shaped who I am in ways I'm still discovering.

Heart

TELL A FRIEND
☐ Tell a friend something you've learned about yourself this year.

SHARE WITH SOMEONE
☐ Share with someone what you're proud of—even if it's quiet or invisible.

MOOD TRACKER

☐	☐	☐	☐	☐	Week 1
☐	☐	☐	☐	☐	Week 2
☐	☐	☐	☐	☐	Week 3
☐	☐	☐	☐	☐	Week 4
☐	☐	☐	☐	☐	Week 5
☐	☐	☐	☐	☐	Week 6
☐	☐	☐	☐	☐	Week 7
☐	☐	☐	☐	☐	Week 8

NOTES:

NOTES:

Draw Your Journey — River or Rollercoaster

Think back over the last few years—not just the move, but everything leading up to it. Life probably hasn't been a straight line. It might've felt more like a river with twists and turns... or a rollercoaster with highs and lows.

Choose one:

🌀 A river — with calm parts, fast parts, obstacles, and new discoveries

🎢 A rollercoaster — with climbs, dips, loops, and moments that took your breath away

🖍️ Draw your journey on a blank page.

You can include:
- Moments of joy
- Times of fear, loss, or confusion
- Turning points or new beginnings
- People who helped you
- Places that mattered
- What you've learned about yourself along the way

📌 There's no right or wrong way to do it—just be honest and creative. This is your story.

Draw Your Journey — River or Rollercoaster

Tip Sheet: Preparing for Life in a New Country

Moving to a new country as a teen comes with big changes and opportunities. Whether you're excited, nervous, or both, this guide is designed to help you settle in with confidence, curiosity, and courage.

🌍 Learn About the Country & Culture
- Explore the country's customs, values, and daily life.
- Learn about typical school routines, popular foods, national holidays, and local sports.
- Follow local influencer's or bloggers to see teen life in real time.

📝 Try this: Make a vision board or digital collage of things you're curious about in your new country.

👥 Understand Teen Culture & Social Norms
- Learn how teens greet each other, what friendships look like, and what's expected in group settings.
- Understand unwritten rules (slang, dress codes, lunch habits, humour).
- Ask safe, trusted locals about what's normal or polite.

📝 Try this: Observe how other teens behave in schools, shops, or parks—what do you notice?

🔊 Language, Slang & Communication
- Get familiar with local slang and idioms—especially if they are English but sound different!
- Practice the local accent or way of speaking. You don't have to change who you are, but understanding helps you fit in.
- Watch teen shows, YouTube channels, or listen to local music.

📝 Try this: Keep a "new words" list in your phone and add phrases as you learn them.

🎤 Music, Style & What's Trending
- Find out what people your age listen to, wear, or follow online.
- Explore local artists, playlists, and styles.
- Check what's trending on social media—but stay true to what you enjoy too.

📝 Try this: Make a playlist that blends your old favourites and new discoveries.

❤️ Emotional Health & Support
- Moving can feel overwhelming. It's okay to grieve what you've left behind and still look forward to what's ahead.
- Talk with someone you trust about how you're really feeling.
- Keep a journal, pray, draw, or find other ways to process your emotions.

📝 Try this: Write down three things you miss and three things you're looking forward to.

⚠️ Safety & Independence
- Learn local emergency numbers and apps.
- Know how to stay safe when out alone or meeting new people.
- Avoid risky areas, especially after dark. Let someone know where you're going.
- Use public transport confidently—know your route and how to ask for help.

📝 Try this: Save emergency contacts in your phone and carry a small ID card with important info.

👮 Talking to Police or Asking for Help
- Know how to identify safe adults: police, teachers, or shop staff.
- In many places, police are there to help—don't be afraid to approach them if you're lost or need assistance.
- Learn what to say clearly and calmly.

📝 Try this: Practice saying: "Hi, I'm new here and I need help finding this place."

💛 Final Thoughts
You don't have to figure everything out right away. Adjusting takes time, and every step you take is part of your journey. Stay open, stay kind to yourself, and remember—you're not alone.
You've got this.

www.ingramcontent.com/pod-product-compliance
Lightning Source LLC
Chambersburg PA
CBHW081417300426
44109CB00020BA/2358